Children
of the
FRONTIER

Sod House   GABL, Photo

Children
of the
FRONTIER

Sylvia Whitman

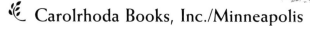

Carolrhoda Books, Inc./Minneapolis

To Selma Masmoudi and her cousins, who I hope will come discover America

Page one: Settlers stand outside their frontier sod house.

Page two: A home in Oklahoma Territory, photographed in the 1890s

Opposite page: This frontier home in North Dakota is covered with tar paper.

Text copyright © 1998 by Sylvia Whitman

Carolrhoda Books, Inc., c/o The Lerner Publishing Group
241 First Avenue North, Minneapolis, MN 55401 U.S.A.

Website address: www.lernerbooks.com

LIBRARY OF CONGRESS CATALOGING-IN-PUBLICATION

Whitman, Sylvia, 1961–
    Children of the frontier / Sylvia Whitman.
        p.   cm. — (Picture the American past)
    Includes bibliographical references and index.
    Summary: Explores the lives of the children of settlers on the American frontier, looking especially at schooling, chores, home life, food, and recreation.
    ISBN 1-57505-240-7
    1. Pioneer children—West (U.S.)—Social life and customs—Juvenile literature. 2. West (U.S.)—Social life and customs—Juvenile literature. 3. Frontier and pioneer life—West (U.S.)—Juvenile literature. [1. Frontier and pioneer life—West (U.S.) 2. West (U.S.)— Social life and customs.] I. Title. II. Series.
F596.W566 1998
977.02'083—dc21   97-33408

Manufactured in the United States of America
1 2 3 4 5 6 – JR – 03 02 01 00 99 98

CONTENTS

Oklahoma. Settlers race to claim land that once belonged to Indians.

Home on the Range

All the past we leave behind . . . .
Pioneers! O pioneers!
—words to a poem by Walt Whitman

On your mark, get set, GO. Land was cheap in the 1800s. The government was even giving it away in some places. Americans hurried to claim a share. Families left homes in the East. Children said good-bye to friends and relatives.

These pioneers brought only what they could fit in a wagon. They settled on the frontier. The frontier was the rough edge of a growing country.

7

Minnesota. Pioneers use logs for their house, barn, and fences.

To keep the free land, settlers had to live on it. First, they needed shelter. In woody areas, they chopped down trees with axes. Children helped grown-ups build cabins in clearings.

Very few trees grew on the prairies of the Midwest. Pioneers crossed acres of long grasses that swayed in the breeze. Every summer new roots tangled with dead roots underground. This made sod. Sod was thick, matted soil that didn't crumble.

Settlers cut sod into blocks, like huge bricks, and stacked them together. A sod house, or "soddy," weighed several tons. A soddy was cool in summer, warm in winter, and fireproof. But creepy. Mice, worms, spiders, and big, brown bullsnakes dropped down from the dirt ceiling.

Nebraska. Moses Speese and his family pose proudly by their sod house.

Sometimes families moved into a hole in a hill. They covered it with boards or sod. Settlers called these cave houses dugouts.

Nebraska. Pioneers find shelter and shade in a dugout.

Utah. The inside of a frontier house could be damp, dark, and crowded—but homey.

Most cabins and dugouts had dirt floors. Above, the roof always leaked. Everybody slept and ate in one room. At one end, a fire burned day and night, summer and winter. The fireplace served as a heater and a cookstove.

Sunlight entered through an open door or a hole cut in the wall. Few cabins had real windows. Most people didn't dare bring glass on the bumpy wagon ride West.

North Dakota. A woman sits surrounded by pictures of her friends and family.

Pioneer mothers tried to make homes cozy. They put up family photographs. They unpacked their treasures—a clock, a mirror, or maybe a birdcage. One lovely thing could brighten up a whole room.

Women and girls did most of the housework. After they swept the floor, they sometimes drew a design with a stick. It made the earth look like a rug. A mother might write "Happy Birthday" in the dirt.

Settlers found decorations in nature. Hunters hung bearskins and deer antlers on the walls. Children picked wildflowers. One girl counted 117 kinds of plants around her house.

Wyoming. Hunting trophies decorate the outside of a log cabin.

Colorado. A girl sprinkles grain for hungry hens.

Hard Rows
To Hoe

How happy am I when I crawl into bed!
A rattlesnake hisses a tune at my head.
—words to a folk song from the 1870s

Parents depended on children to help the family survive. Even young children fed chickens, herded sheep, and milked cows. One woman who grew up on the frontier remembers, "Everybody worked; it was a part of life, for there was no life without it."

Families knew they had to work hard to succeed. If they failed, they would have to turn around and head back East—unless they starved to death first.

Kansas. A family milks the cows.

Pioneers relied on animals for food, clothes, and transportation. Pigs became bacon. Sheep gave wool. Horses pulled wagons and plows.

Most settlers had little money. If they needed cash to buy something, they sold eggs or maybe a cow. Animals were so valuable that in bad weather a family might bring them into the house. One farmer woke up after a storm without any pants— his calf had eaten them!

People and animals needed water as much as food. Sometimes a stream ran through the land. If not, a girl or boy might drive a wagon to a spring and fill a barrel with water.

Montana. Genevra Fornell fetches water. Because water was so precious, many families took baths just once a week.

Kansas. A brother and sister give water to a thirsty horse. Many frontier children learned how to ride before they could read.

Most families tried to dig wells. Then they pumped the water trapped underground. As soon as children could lift a bucket, they were carrying water into the house.

Another daily job was collecting fuel for the fire. Children picked up twigs or stripped bark from trees. On the prairie, they gathered bones or animal droppings. They brought buffalo and cow manure home in wheelbarrows or sacks. Sometimes children carried the hard, dry chips on their heads.

Buffalo chips didn't smell that bad. Burning, they were no worse than bones.

Kansas. A woman collects buffalo and cow chips for burning.

Chores never ended. In the garden, children pulled weeds and scared away crows. In the fields, they cut tall stalks of wheat and rye. In the woods, they shot rabbits and turkeys. They fished in creeks and gathered walnuts under trees.

Idaho. A boy goes hunting with his dog and his air rifle.

Idaho. A boy named Lyle Brace bakes sourdough biscuits.

At home, children sifted cornmeal and baked biscuits. They made candles by pouring boiling animal fat into molds.

Frontier families worked and worked. Sometimes they didn't see their neighbors for weeks. A 15-year-old girl in Texas wrote, "It is so misirably lonesome here. I feel burried alive . . ."

Colorado. Boys pitch hay and illustrate the old saying "Many hands make light work."

Jobs went faster thanks to brothers and sisters.

Brothers and sisters also found ways to have fun. Children carved whistles out of willow branches and made dolls out of corn husks. They turned boxes into wagons. At night, they played seven-up, dominoes, and checkers.

Idaho. Hollis and Nadine Murray ride in a wagon pulled by a ram.

When things went right, families celebrated. Everybody took a break to taste a good melon.

Sometimes everything went wrong. Too much or too little rain could ruin crops. Grasshoppers and locusts sometimes ate the corn down to the ground. These bugs also chewed ropes, harnesses, and mattresses. They fell into wells and spoiled the water. One girl said the locusts sounded "like a train of cars on a railroad."

Colorado. A farm family enjoys fresh melon from the garden.

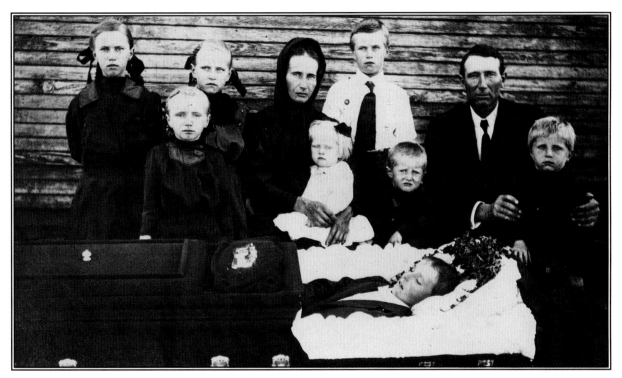

Oklahoma. The family of Leonard Meget gathers sadly around his coffin. Leonard was 13 when he died.

Pioneers faced danger everywhere. Lightning struck during summer storms. Wildfires burned up the prairies. Poisonous snakes slithered through cracks in the walls. A man in Kansas killed 133 rattlesnakes on his farm one year.

The worst killer was disease. In one family, six children died in a single month. When a child came down with a fever, parents worried and prayed. Sometimes an older brother or sister rode to fetch a doctor.

North Dakota. Friends stitch a quilt. The pattern is called double Irish chain.

Neighbors shared sorrows and joys. Settlers met to roll logs, butcher pigs, and sew quilts. While their hands worked, they talked or sang songs.

Montana. The Deem family prepares to pick berries on Bearpaw Mountain. Some chores didn't seem like work.

Women and children spent several days a year gathering wild berries. They picked and ate until their hands and lips turned purple. Sometimes they camped in the woods. They brought sugar and jars to can the berries for winter. Back home, they baked pies and made wine.

Minnesota. Young children attended school more often than their older brothers and sisters, who sometimes stayed at home to help with the heavy work of the farm.

Taming the Wild West

Go West, young man, and grow up with the country.
—written by Horace Greeley,
a newspaperman, in 1850

The first years on the frontier were the hardest and loneliest for families. But more people kept moving West. Parents joined together to build schools.

Schools looked like the houses in the area—cabins, soddies, or dugouts. Usually the children all studied in one room.

Colorado. A teacher leads a reading lesson.

Children often learned to read at home, usually from the Bible. They practiced at school. They also studied math, spelling, history, and geography.

Sometimes the teacher split students into small groups. It was hard to teach 5-year-olds and 15-year-olds at the same time. Older children helped younger ones.

Schools followed the farm calendar. They closed when parents needed children in the fields. Students walked several miles to school. Because of snowstorms, sickness, or chores, they often missed days.

Even at school, children couldn't escape work. They had to fetch water and chop wood for the stove.

North Dakota. A stove heats a frontier school.

Minnesota. Girls play in front of their school.

Most frontier children liked school. It gave them a chance to make friends. At recess, students played ring-around-the-rosy and pop-the-whip.

Anti-I-Over was a popular game. One team threw a ball over a wall or a wagon and yelled "Anti!" If the other team caught the ball, they ran around and tried to tag the throwers.

Idaho. Children bring sleds to church in winter.

On Sundays, children enjoyed seeing friends and neighbors at church. Often the service was long. Everyone looked forward to dinner and visits afterward.

Many frontier families rested on Sunday afternoons. They did only a few chores. Settlers read newspapers and magazines. They wrote letters to people back East. Then they didn't feel so lonely and far away.

Utah. Family members spend a quiet September Sunday reading.

Colorado. Stores fill the gaps between schools and churches in Black Hawk.

Children loved going to town. They listened to men gossip as the blacksmith pounded out horseshoes. They watched ladies try to keep their long skirts out of the mud. Sometimes their parents bought them lemon drops or rock candy at the general store.

Kansas. Shoppers cross muddy streets on wooden planks.

Pioneers built towns with animals in mind. Main Street was wide, so farmers could make U-turns with horse-drawn wagons. At least one stable in town sold hay. Riders tied horses to hitching posts outside stores. Storekeepers made high, wooden sidewalks so families could load their wagons easily.

By 1900, Americans had reached the end of the frontier. They had settled the West all the way to the Pacific Ocean. There were still wild places, but they were harder to find.

Frontier families believed they had helped make the United States a great country. They felt proud. Settlers held parades on the Fourth of July. Towns threw parties on their birthdays.

Pioneers wanted everyone to remember their struggle.

Idaho. Children in Silver City ride on a Fourth of July parade wagon.

Settlers continued to work hard. But they also had more time to relax. Everybody enjoyed picnics. On weekends, town and farm families rode into the country. When they found a quiet spot, they spread a blanket and ate lunch.

Idaho. Picnickers rest after lunch.

Idaho. Campers "rough it" in the woods.

Parents also took children camping. How things had changed!
Once settlers had missed the safety of the East. Now they missed
the challenge of the frontier. Sleeping in tents and cooking over
fires, Americans felt like pioneers again.

Frontier Food

A Recipe for Johnnycakes

My clothes are all ragged as my language is rough.
My bread is corn dodgers, both solid and tough.
But yet I am happy and live at my ease
On sorghum molasses, bacon, and cheese.
—words to "The Lane County Bachelor"

Pioneers didn't have time for fancy cooking. There was too much work to do. In the early days of the frontier, many families didn't sit down together for meals. The women prepared the food, put it on the table, and people ate when they could.

Pioneers grew grain for themselves and their animals. They baked breads with wheat, barley, rye, and corn. Pioneers ate a lot of corn because it could grow almost anywhere.

Settlers made all sorts of goodies out of cornmeal. Corn dodgers were small cakes usually fried hard. Hoecakes got their name because people baked them on the metal face of a hoe heated in hot ashes. A similar—and very popular—snack was called a johnnycake.

Johnnycakes cooked quickly on a board set beside the fire. People slipped them into their pockets for long trips. No one knows for certain how johnnycakes got their name. Maybe they were "journey" cakes.

People baked johnnycakes in the oven or over an open fire. In this recipe, you will cook them on the stovetop, like pancakes.

JOHNNYCAKES

1 cup cornmeal
1/2 teaspoon baking soda
1/2 teaspoon salt
1 tablespoon butter*
3/4 cup water
1/2 cup buttermilk*
butter
maple or fruit syrup, honey, or warm meat gravy to taste

1. In a medium-sized bowl, mix cornmeal, baking soda, and salt. Use a spoon to form a well, or depression, in the middle. Using a table knife, cut butter into small pieces and place in well.

2. Pour water into a kettle. Warm over high heat until it boils. Then ask an adult to measure boiling water and pour over mixture in bowl, while you stir until butter is melted. Continue stirring to get rid of lumps.

*In place of butter, many frontier cooks—particularly those who did not own their own cows and have a ready supply of milk or butter—used bacon fat or other meat drippings. Cooks also substituted water for buttermilk when buttermilk was not available.

3. Add buttermilk, continuing to stir well. Batter will have the consistency of heavy pancake batter.

4. Grease a large pan or griddle with butter. Heat on medium. Drop batter into pan a tablespoon at a time. Cook about 10 minutes until brown and crisp underneath. Flip johnnycakes and let them brown on the other side. Add more butter to griddle if needed.

5. Serve warm with maple or fruit syrup, honey, or warm meat gravy.

Makes about 15 johnnycakes. Serves 4 to 5.
Note: If stored in an airtight container in a refrigerator, batter will keep for 2 to 3 days.
Leftover cooked johnnycakes can be reheated in a microwave oven.

NOTE TO TEACHERS AND ADULTS

For children, frontier times sometimes seem like part of a far-off past. But there are many ways to make the frontier and its people come alive. Along with helping children cook up that frontier staple, johnnycakes, you can explore America's frontier past in other ways. One way is to read more about the frontier, and more books on the topic are listed on pages 45 and 46. Another way to explore the past is to train young readers to study historical photographs. Historical photographs hold many clues about how life was lived in earlier times.

Ask your children or students to look for the details and "read" all the information in each picture in this book. For example, how is the front yard shown on page 8 different from a typical modern front yard? (Most modern yards aren't filled with logs. When settlers cleared the land, they used the cut trees to make their homes, barns, and fences and to warm their homes in winter.) Why are animal skins tacked on the cabin walls in the photograph on page 13? (Many settlers didn't have money to pay for things, so they traded crops they grew or the skins of animals they killed for goods from traders or from a general store.) To better learn to read historical photographs, have young readers try these activities:

Chore Time
Look at the pictures of children doing their chores on the frontier. On a piece of paper in one column, under the heading "frontier days," make a list of the chores being done. In another column, under the heading "my parents' day," list chores your parents did when they were little. (Set aside time after school or on a weekend to interview your parents about their chores.)

In a third column, under the heading "today," list the chores you have to do each week. In a final column, under the heading "tomorrow," try to imagine the kinds of chores your own children will have to do.

A Log Cabin Home

Compare the cabins shown on pages 8 and 13 with descriptions of how a log cabin is made in *Little House on the Prairie* or in *Log Cabin in the Woods* (see pages 45 and 46). How do the cabins in the photos differ from that described in the story? Based on the details you see in the photographs, what conclusions can you draw about the people who lived in these frontier cabins?

Writing Letters

From the perspective of a new settler living in one of the frontier homes shown in this book, write a letter to a friend or family member "back East" telling of your new life. What are the differences between your life on the frontier and the life you left behind in more settled lands? What do you miss most? What do you like most about your new life? How soon will you be able to get to a town and mail your letter?

Growing Up on the Frontier

Dress in costume and tell your friends, parents, or classmates what it was like to grow up on the frontier. Read the text—and the photos—in this book for information and for details about daily life. To give your presentation more authenticity, read some of the books on frontier life listed on pages 45 and 46. You may wish to act out the part of Essie from *Grandma Essie's Covered Wagon* or Ollie from *Log Cabin in the Woods* or that of a young settler in Nicodemus, Kansas, as described in *Going Home to Nicodemus.*

Resources on the American Frontier

Chu, Daniel and Bill Shaw. *Going Home to Nicodemus: The Story of an African American Frontier Town and the Pioneers Who Settled It.* Morristown, N.J.: Julian Messner, published by Silver Burdett Press, 1994. This book tells the story of a frontier town, Nicodemus, Kansas, and the former slaves who built it.

Duncan, Dayton. *The West: An Illustrated History for Children.* New York: Little, Brown and Company, 1996. One of three companion books to the PBS television series of the same name, this volume combines historical photographs with the stories of the many different people who lived in the American West.

Hakim, Joy. *Liberty for All?* New York: Oxford University Press, 1994. Part of a series of books covering the history of the United States, this volume focuses on the years 1815 to 1861, a time of settlement on the frontier.

Henry, Joanne Landers. Illustrated by Joyce Audy Zarins. *Log Cabin in the Woods: A True Story about a Pioneer Boy.* New York: Four Winds Press, 1988. Landers follows a year in the life of a real frontier boy, Ollie Johnson, who lived in the woods of central Indiana in the 1830s.

Miller, Brandon Marie. *Buffalo Gals: Women of the Old West.* Minneapolis, Minn.: Lerner Publications Company, 1995. Using excerpts from diaries, letters, and travel guides, Miller paints a picture of the lives of girls and women on the western frontier.

Turner, Ann. Illustrated by Ronald Himler. *Dakota Dugout.* New York: Macmillan Publishing Company, 1985. Turner's brief text turns the sights and sounds of a harsh and lonely prairie into poetry, while Himler's drawings bring out the details of frontier life.

Walker, Barbara. *The Little House Cookbook: Frontier Foods from Laura Ingalls Wilder's Classic Stories.* New York: Harper and Row, 1979. Walker presents recipes and fascinating facts about the foods eaten in the Little House books written by Laura Ingalls Wilder.

Wilder, Laura Ingalls. *Little House on the Prairie.* New York: Harper and Row Publishers, 1935. Laura and her family move from the Big Woods of Wisconsin to Indian Territory in what is now Oklahoma. There, the family builds a cabin and discovers the hard work, fun, and excitement of life on the frontier.

Williams, David. Illustrated by Wiktor Sadowski. *Grandma Essie's Covered Wagon.* New York: Alfred A. Knopf, 1993. In this picture book, the author records his grandmother's memories of life—with all its ups and downs—on the frontier in Kansas, Oklahoma, and Missouri.

Websites about the Frontier

http://www.pbs.org/weta/thewest
Designed to give viewers of the PBS television series *The West,* access to more information, this Website provides biographies of people mentioned on the series.

http://www.nara.gov:70/inform/dc/audvis/still/amwest.html
Photographs of the American West from the collections of the National Archives in Washington, D.C., are available for viewing here.

New Words

buffalo chips: dried buffalo manure, often used as fuel for a fire

dugout: a cavelike shelter dug out of the side of a hill. Settlers often used logs to hold up the sides and roof of a dugout.

frontier: the rough edge of a growing country. In the United States, the frontier marked the border between land that people mainly of European background had settled and land they had not yet settled. By about 1900, most frontier lands had been settled.

sod: thick, matted soil that sticks together. Roots of grass tangle like hair underground and hold the dirt in place.

soddy: a house made from huge bricks of sod

Index

TIMELINE

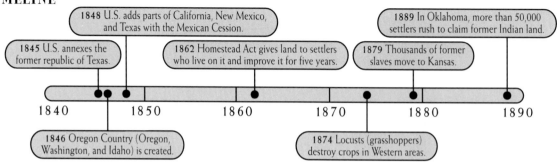

1848 U.S. adds parts of California, New Mexico, and Texas with the Mexican Cession.

1845 U.S. annexes the former republic of Texas.

1862 Homestead Act gives land to settlers who live on it and improve it for five years.

1889 In Oklahoma, more than 50,000 settlers rush to claim former Indian land.

1879 Thousands of former slaves move to Kansas.

1840   1850   1860   1870   1880   1890

1846 Oregon Country (Oregon, Washington, and Idaho) is created.

1874 Locusts (grasshoppers) destroy crops in Western areas.

ABOUT THE AUTHOR

Sylvia Whitman lives with her husband in Orlando, Florida, and works as a learning specialist at Rollins College. She has degrees in folklore and mythology, American studies, and creative writing. Her publications for children include a half dozen history books and articles in such magazines as *Cobblestone, Cricket,* and *Jack and Jill.* An amateur photographer, she loves to work with images as well as words.

"If I had been born a hundred years earlier," she says, "I might have set out in a wagon with my husband to raise a family on the frontier. I love adventures. But I also love books and all the comforts of home. I try to imagine myself in a lonely cabin fighting off hungry grasshoppers with my broom. Would I have been brave and strong enough to help build a house, a farm, and maybe a whole town from scratch?"

PHOTO ACKNOWLEDGMENTS

The photographs in this book are reproduced through the courtesy of: Colorado Historical Society, front cover, pp. 14, 15, 22, 24; Western History Collections, University of Oklahoma Library, back cover, pp. 2, 25; Saskatchewan Archives Board, photograph no. R-A492-1, p. 1; State Historical Society of North Dakota, pp. 5, 7, 12, 26, 31; Oklahoma Territorial Museum, Oklahoma Historical Society, p. 6; Minnesota Historical Society, pp. 8, 28, 32; Solomon D. Butcher Collection, Nebraska State Historical Society, p. 9; Nebraska State Historical Society, p. 10; Used by permission, Utah State Historical Society, all rights reserved, pp. 11, 34; Wyoming State Museum, p. 13; The Kansas State Historical Society, pp. 16, 18, 19, 36; Montana Historical Society, Helena, pp. 17, 27; Idaho State Historical Society, pp. 20 (#60-139.23), 21 (#77-137.1), 23 (#79-63.6), 33 (#62-108.36/C), 37 (#77-19.20), 38 (#60-139.17), 39 (#73-129.21); Library of Congress, p. 29; Denver Public Library, Western History Department, pp. 30, 35.